The Reminiscences Of
Admiral John S. McCain, Jr.
U.S. Navy (Retired)

Interviewed By
John T. Mason, Jr.

U.S. Naval Institute • Annapolis, Maryland

Copyright © 1999

Preface

In the mid-1970s my predecessor, Dr. John T. Mason, Jr., sat down with recently retired Admiral John S. McCain, Jr., for what was intended to be a series of oral history interviews covering the admiral's entire life and naval service. For whatever reason, the admiral did no more interviews after this first one. The good news is that he did not stick strictly to the chronological approach in telling of his life history. As a result, the reader gets bits and snippets of various aspects of his career, his sense of values on honor and leadership, and insights into his famous father, who was also a wartime admiral.

The interviewee's son is retired Navy Captain John S. McCain III, a Vietnam War prisoner and later a member of Congress. As of this writing, Senator McCain is running for the presidency. Last year, Senator McCain authorized the release of his father's oral history interview and thus made it available for public use. The first use was by McCain's own coauthor, Mark Salter, who used it in helping the senator fashion a memoir of his family's three generations of naval officers. Thus material from this interview appears in Senator McCain's book <u>Faith of My Fathers</u>, published earlier this year by Random House.

In the course of moving from the initial raw transcript of the oral interview, I have done virtually no editing. It appears here almost word for word as the admiral related it to Dr. Mason. I have added footnotes to provide additional background information. Ms. Ann Hassinger of the Naval Institute's history division has made a significant contribution through her diligence in the overall process of printing, proofreading, and overseeing the binding of the completed volume.

Paul Stillwell
Director, History Division
U.S. Naval Institute
December 1999

Admiral John S. McCain, Jr., U.S. Navy (Retired)

John Sidney, McCain, Jr., was born in Council Bluffs, Iowa, on 17 January 1911, son of Mrs. John S. (Katherine Vaulx) McCain and the late Admiral McCain, USN. He attended Central High School in Washington, D.C., prior to his appointment (at large) to the U.S. Naval Academy, Annapolis, Maryland, in 1927. He was graduated and commissioned ensign on 4 June 1931 and subsequently promoted to the rank of admiral, to date from 1 May 1967.

From June 1931, he served for two years in the USS Oklahoma (BB-37), a unit of Battleship Division One, Battle Force. He reported in July 1933 for instruction in submarines at the Naval Submarine Base, New London, Groton, Connecticut. After completing the course in December of that year, he served successively in the USS S-45 (SS-156) of Submarine Force, Pearl Harbor, and the USS R-13 (SS-90) of Submarine Division Four, attached to the Naval Submarine Base, New London.

From June 1938 until May 1940, McCain served as an instructor in the Department of Electrical Engineering at the Naval Academy. Following duty at the Naval Academy, he served in the submarine Skipjack (SS-184) until April 1941. He next reported as prospective commanding officer of the USS O-8 (SS-69), which was being refitted in the Philadelphia Navy Yard. He commanded her from her recommissioning until May 1942.

Ordered to the Electric Boat Company, Groton, Connecticut, he was in charge of fitting out the USS Gunnel (SS-253) and assumed command of that submarine at her commissioning on 20 August 1942. Under his command, the Gunnel arrived at Fedala, French Morocco, a few days before the D-Day bombardment, in time to photograph the proposed beachhead and make a general reconnaissance of Casablanca and Fedala. Later, he took Gunnel to the Pacific, where she sank an enemy destroyer and sank or damaged additional Japanese shipping.

On 14 July 1944 he was ordered to New London, where he served briefly before reporting in October to the Electric Boat Company, to fit out another submarine, the USS Dentuda (SS-335). He served as commanding officer during her first and only war patrol in the Pacific, turning over command of the Dentuda at the cessation of hostilities in August 1945. For service in combat during World War II, he was awarded the Silver Star Medal, the Bronze Star Medal with combat V and two letters of commendation. One letter of commendation came from Commander in Chief U.S. Atlantic Fleet; the other was from Commander in Chief U.S. Pacific Fleet.

Returning to the United States in November 1945, McCain served in the Bureau of Naval Personnel, Navy Department, Washington, D.C., as Director of Records until January 1949. Again ordered to duty afloat, he commanded Submarine Division 71 for 11 months and then commanded Submarine Division 51 for two months. In February 1950 he joined the heavy cruiser St. Paul (CA-73) as executive officer and in November of that year returned to the Navy Department. Reporting to the officer of the Deputy Chief of Naval Operations (Operations), he served as director of the Undersea Warfare Research and Development Branch until March 1953, when he became Commander Submarine Squadron Six.

In July 1954 he assumed command of the attack transport Monrovia (APA-31), and in May 1955 was detached to report to duty as director of the Progress Analysis Group in the office of the Chief of Naval Operations. From October 1957 to April 1958, he was commanding officer of the heavy cruiser Albany (CA-123). He was then detached for duty in the office of the Chief of Naval Operations. On 23 June 1958 he reported as Chief, Legislative Liaison, Executive Officer of the Secretary of the Navy, and on 9 November of that year was promoted to rear admiral. On 10 August 1960 he became Commander Amphibious Group Two, and on 26 May 1961 he assumed duties of Commander Amphibious Training Command, Atlantic Fleet.

In September 1962 Admiral McCain reported as Chief of Information, Navy Department, Washington, D.C. He left that post one ear later to assume, as vice admiral, the duties of Commander Amphibious Force, Atlantic Fleet. While serving in that post, the admiral received his first Legion of Merit for his leadership of naval forces in the Caribbean during the crisis in the Dominican Republic. He received a gold star in lieu of a Second Legion of Merit for his outstanding performance as Commander Amphibious Force Atlantic Fleet.

In June 1965 he reported as vice chairman of the delegation to the United Nations Military Staff Committee in New York. At the same time he became Commander Eastern Sea Frontier and Commander Atlantic Reserve Fleet. In October 1966, with the reorganization of the reserve fleets, he was relieved of the latter command. Immediately prior to his detachment as vice chairman of the U.S./U.N. Delegation, Military Staff Committee, in April 1967, he was awarded a gold star in lieu of his third Legion of Merit. The medal was for meritorious service during the period July 1965 to April 1967 while serving in that post.

After being detached in April, he assumed the duties of Commander in Chief U.S. Naval Forces Europe on 1 May 1967. For exceptionally meritorious service in that capacity from April 1967 to July 1968 he was awarded the Distinguished Service Medal. On 31 July 1968 he became Commander in Chief Pacific and held that billet until 1 September 1972. For that duty he received a gold star in lieu of a second Distinguished Service Medal. In September 1972 he reported as a special assistant to the Chief of Naval Operations and served as such while relieved of active duty, pending his retirement, effective 1 November of that year. He died on 22 March 1981.

In addition to the already mentioned decorations, Admiral McCain held the American Defense Service Medal, Fleet Clasp; American Campaign Medal; European-African-Middle Eastern Campaign Medal with engagement star; Asiatic-Pacific Campaign Medal with three stars; World War II Victory Medal; Navy Occupation Service Medal; National Defense Service Medal with bronze star; Korean

Service Medal; Armed Forces Expeditionary Medal; and the United Nations Service Medal. He also had the Korean Presidential Unit Citation badge.

Admiral and Mrs. McCain, the former Roberta Wright of Los Angeles, had three children: Mrs. Jean McCain Flather, Captain John Sidney McCain III, and Joseph Pinckney McCain.

Authorization

The U.S. Naval Institute is hereby authorized to make available to individuals, libraries, and other repositories of its choosing the transcripts of an oral history interview concerning the life and naval career of the late Admiral John S. McCain, Jr., U.S. Navy (Retired). The interview was recorded by Admiral McCain on 6 January 1975 in collaboration with Dr. John T. Mason, Jr., for the U.S. Naval Institute.

The undersigned does hereby release and assign to the U.S. Naval Institute the rights and title to this interview, with the exception that the undersigned retains the right to use the material for his own purposes, as he sees fit. The copyright in both the oral and transcribed versions shall be the sole property of the U.S. Naval Institute. The tape recording of the interview is and will remain the property of the U.S. Naval Institute.

Signed and sealed this ___17TH___ day of ___JUNE___ 1998.

John S. McCain III
for the estate of John S. McCain, Jr.

District of Columbia :ss:

Subscribed and sworn to before me this 17TH day of JUNE 1998.

Notary Public, DC

MY COMMISSION EXPIRES APRIL 14, 1999

Interview with Admiral John S. McCain, Jr., U.S. Navy (Retired)

Place: Admiral McCain's office in Washington, D.C.

Date: Monday, 6 January 1975

Interviewer: John T. Mason, Jr.

John T. Mason: It's a delight to meet you. I've been looking forward to the possibility of this series for a long, long time. And now we begin chapter one. Would you begin, sir, in the proper way with a biography, by telling me the date and place of your birth and something about your famous Navy background?

Admiral McCain: Strange as it may seem, I was born in Council Bluffs, Iowa.[*] My mother's family comes from Arkansas, my father's family from Mississippi.[†] And the reason I was born in Council Bluffs is because my father was then the engineering officer on the old armored cruiser San Diego, which was on one of these extended cruises around the southern tip of South America.[‡] And my mother went up there to stay with a sister who had moved into that area. That's when McCain—this generation—made his first appearance on the face of this earth.

But a great part of my time was actually spent living as a boy in Washington, D.C., because of the fact that my father had so much duty in this city when the old Navy Department used to be down there on Constitution Avenue instead of over in that great big, complicated, strange affair called the Pentagon building. But I lived within, I say, a block and a half of where I'm living now, at 2325 20th Street, N.W. I can even remember the address that I lived. I used to deliver newspapers in the apartment house in which I am now living. And I wanted to go to the Naval Academy from the time that I was old enough to begin to realize there was such.

---

[*] His birth was on 17 January 1911.
[†] For more on the family's background, see John S. McCain III, Faith of My Fathers (New York: Random House, 1999).
[‡] The record of his father, John S. McCain, who was then a junior officer in the Navy, indicates he did not serve in the San Diego until 1915-18. From the autumn of 1909 to February 1912, the senior McCain served in the armored cruiser Washington.

John T. Mason: Naturally, there was no other thought, I suppose.

Admiral McCain: That's right. And so I went to both grammar school and high school here in Washington, D.C.

John T. Mason: Yes, you were in that famous Central High School, weren't you?

Admiral McCain: That's right.

John T. Mason: Do you still belong to the alumni association?

Admiral McCain: I certainly do. Much to my astonishment, they gave me an award about three or four months ago, I guess it was, maybe six months ago, of being one of the outstanding graduates of the school.

John T. Mason: Well, great. They should have.

Admiral McCain: But in any event, from Central, I went to a very famous preparatory school, and I've often wondered what happened to it. It was called under two names. One was Shadman's, and the other was the Columbia Preparatory School, which was the more formal name for it. They only had a student body of about 45 or 50 down there, and they prepared young men for both the Naval Academy and West Point.

It was a very tough, demanding school, and it stood me in good stead in the years after that because of the habits of study which were instilled into a boy of my age. And I say "boy," because I went to the Naval Academy shortly after I turned 16, which is the youngest you could get into the school. And the preceding year, I was subjected to the ideas, the philosophies, and the habits of study which Shadman was more than capable of instilling into young people.

John T. Mason: It's an ideal way in which to prepare for the Naval Academy.

Admiral McCain: Oh, yes, and I had to take, of course, a competitive examination for a presidential appointment.

John T. Mason: This was a nationwide competition.

Admiral McCain: Absolutely. And they took the top 20, and I stood about two or three in that group, which is the last time I have shone scholastically since I can remember, see. But the school was outstanding, and some day I'm going to check to see what ever happened to that outfit. It would very nearly guarantee any boy that if he took a nine-month course in this school, that he would get into either West Point or the Naval Academy, regardless of whether it was a competitive examination or it was a direct appointment from a congressman or a senator.

John T. Mason: Wasn't it located on New Hampshire Avenue?

Admiral McCain: No, it was located down there on Rhode Island Avenue. There weren't too many people that had heard of this school, really, except us few who were subjected to the rigors of it. But at the time that I went, it was *the* outstanding prep school in the country from the standard of record.

Now, he had an old house that he set this up in, and Mr. Shadman was not one to spend money, so the house itself was not of the highest order. And we used such things as, oh, the living room and the dining room and a bedroom upstairs for classrooms. All the furniture had been removed, of course. But, as I say, the whole school was set up for one purpose, and that was to get boys into the Naval Academy and West Point and teach them the basics of study and hard work.

John T. Mason: Once you got this presidential appointment, did it permit you an interview with the President?

Admiral McCain: No, indeed. I never even got near the President. [Chuckle] The next thing after that, of course, was the physical exam at the Naval Academy, and then we went right on in from there to midshipmen.

John T. Mason: Lapping back for just a second, you said that earlier, as a boy, you had a newspaper route. This indicates some parental control over your development.

Admiral McCain: I hope to shout I had parental control. My mother was the real parental control, because my father was gone part of the time that I was growing up. And my mother was very well-founded in those principles that young people ought to be brought up in if they're going to be a success in life later, see. And as a matter of fact, her father was an Episcopalian minister, and she had all the background that went with this type of life.

When my father was home, of course, why—he was there a big part of the time, too, but most of his time was spent down at the Navy Department.

John T. Mason: Yes, a Navy mother has to serve as both mother and father to the offspring most of the time, doesn't she?

Admiral McCain: Yes, but my father recognized this sort of thing, too, in his absence from home. Every summer that the situation permitted, why, he would take my brother and myself on a camping trip. I must admit—they were some awful camping trips we went on because there were no practical McCains on this camping trip.

But just before I went into the Naval Academy and after I had passed the physical exam and the mental exams, I went out to Bremerton Navy Yard because, again, my father was away that whole year that I was prepping for the Naval Academy.[*] He was then executive officer of the old battleship New Mexico, and it was in overhaul in the Bremerton Navy Yard.[†] So I went out there, and I spent two weeks with him aboard that

---

[*] Puget Sound Navy Yard, Bremerton, Washington.
[†] The senior McCain served as executive officer of the battleship New Mexico (BB-40) from September 1926 to April 1928.

ship of his, the New Mexico, as a final and farewell gesture before I went into the Naval Academy.

John T. Mason: Maybe this would be the point to ask you to talk a little bit about your father.

Admiral McCain: My father was a very—he was a great leader, first, and people loved him, and he knew how to lead. He also knew when the time came to be a strict disciplinarian, versus the time to be a more easygoing commanding officer. And he had an intense and keen sense of humor. My mother used to say about him that the blood of life flowed through his veins, he was so keenly interested in people and this sort of thing. In fact, it wasn't too long after that that he went to Pensacola and went into naval air.[*]

But he was also, amongst other things, extraordinarily well read. Now, by that I mean as a boy he had read such things as Shakespeare and all the rest of these things that they try—or did at that time, anyway, encourage young people to engage in. So also this gave to him an outstanding command of the English language, which will stand you in good stead, I can assure you, as time moves on. I don't have to tell you about the fact that he was a man of great moral and physical courage. The fact that he had the fast carrier task force under Halsey bears witness to that.[†]

Now, I was in submarines all during the war, and the day they signed the peace treaty, they took a number of United States submarine commanding officers like myself and the crews of our submarines and transferred us to Japanese submarines which had surrendered.[‡] And we tied up alongside the United States tender, Proteus, in Tokyo Bay. And right after they signed the peace treaty, my father came over to the Proteus.

---

[*] The senior McCain entered flight training at Pensacola, Florida, in June 1935 and got his wings as a naval aviator in August 1936 at the age of 52.
[†] In 1944-45, as a vice admiral, McCain commanded Task Force 38 in the Pacific under Admiral William F. Halsey, Jr., USN, who commanded the Third Fleet.
[‡] The battleship Missouri (BB-63) was the site of the Japanese signing of surrender documents in Tokyo Bay on 2 September 1945. John McCain, Jr., commanded the submarine Dentuda (SS-335) from the time of commissioning in 1944 until he was relieved in August 1945.

John S. McCain, Jr. (1/6/75) – Page 6

Admiral Lockwood, who was then Commander Submarines Pacific, had a luncheon.[*] And during the process of this luncheon, I got my father off to one side, and I said to him that I would like to talk to him alone in that little stateroom they used to give commanding officers on submarine tenders when they had command of a submarine that was tied up alongside. And we went back there, and we talked for a little while. And he was to every—and I knew him as well as anybody in this world, with the possible exception of my mother—he looked in fine health to me. And God knows his conversation was anything but that indicative of a man who was sick. And two days later he died of a heart attack.[†]

That taught me a lesson in life, too, and that is, you cannot tell how a good man feels unless he wants to let you know how he feels, and that's it. The only thing I do know is that he and Mitscher and men of that stature were very tired when the war was over, for obvious reasons. And strangely enough, Mitscher died of the same sort of a heart attack a year, to the day, later, after my father had passed on.[‡]

John T. Mason: They were really casualties of the war.

Admiral McCain: Absolutely. Without any question, they were casualties of the war. And my father said to me at that time, he said, "Son, there is no greater thing than to die for the principles—for the country and the principles that you believe in." And that was one part of the conversation that came through—and I have remembered down through the years—with him at that time. And I considered myself very fortunate to have had a chance to see him at that particular moment.

John T. Mason: Indeed, yes.

---

[*] Vice Admiral Charles A. Lockwood, Jr., USN, served as Commander Submarines Pacific Fleet from February 1943 to December 1945.
[†] McCain, Sr., died on 6 September 1945 while at home in California. He had been scheduled to serve as Deputy Director of the Veterans Administration. An act of Congress promoted him posthumously to four-star admiral.
[‡] Admiral Marc A. Mitscher, USN, was serving as Commander in Chief Atlantic Fleet when he suffered a heart attack on Sunday, 26 January 1947, his 60th birthday. He died on 3 February. For details, see the Naval Institute oral history of Captain Frederick A. Edwards, Sr., who was on Mitscher's staff at the time.

Admiral McCain: You see, they flew us all the way from Guam. There were a whole bunch of us submarine skippers who went up there. Our submarines were in Guam. They called us back in, so I was lucky to go up into Tokyo Bay to get command of this Japanese submarine.

John T. Mason: Well, sir, shall we go back now to the Naval Academy and the entrance there?

Admiral McCain: Yes, indeed.

John T. Mason: You had an awfully good idea what to expect at the academy.

Admiral McCain: Well, you can always have a good idea what to expect, but what you expect and what actually takes place can be an entirely unrelated subject. The point I'm trying to make is that it's awfully hard to describe to a man what some physical, spiritual, and mental transformations or rigors he may be going under, without him actually going through the process himself. And it was quite something.

Now, in those days, of course, in the Unites States there was great respect for the military, much more so than there was in later years in my experience. This was before the armed services of the United States in World War II became such a massive organization, and that always leads to a certain deterioration in a thing called morale and respect.

But in any event, I went in there at the age of 16, and I weighed 105 pounds. I could hardly carry a Springfield rifle, which they used to drill us with extensively, and also particularly when it came time for cutter drill. Getting out there and holding an oar was another unique experience in my life. But the whole training system at the Naval Academy was good.

Now, it wasn't the intellectual tack that one might expect to get from Oxford, though in many respects it far exceeded Oxford, in that it did the very thing that Oxford tries to do, and that is inject into us young men and boys who were coming along, a sense of discipline—internal discipline, which you've got to have in life if you're going to really do the job properly.

John T. Mason: You use that as a framework on which to build.

Admiral McCain: That's right. And that's why when you graduate from the Naval Academy, it's highly incumbent on these young officers that they continue to read and continue to absorb from their betters that have gone before them, see. I heard some man make a statement one time not so long ago that the fact of reading the lives of great men was somewhat a waste of time because this was past history. Well, this is stupid on the face of it, because one of the real factors of life is what you learn from reading about the lives of great men, because there are certain fundamentals of human relationships that never change, regardless of what.

And so, anyway, I entered plebe year on June the sixth of 1927.[*] Plebe year was rather pleasant compared with what came later when the upper classmen got back.

John T. Mason: [Laughter] Still the days of hazing, was it?

Admiral McCain: Oh, yes. And hazing is a good thing if it's properly controlled, which it was in those days, because it taught a respect for higher authority that you wouldn't get otherwise. One of the big disadvantages to hazing, as you and I both know, that is the immaturity of the hazer sometimes may lead to transgressions and excesses which are not of the best, but on the other hand, hazing is all right.

They used to make us walk down the center of the corridor and, as we used the expression, take a brace at formation, that is, stand up specifically and particularly straight with the chin tucked in and this sort of business. And they were made to sit on three inches of the chair and were very specific about how we held the fork and the knife and all the rest of these. And in reflection, there's good reason for that, too, because the entering class at the Naval Academy, regardless of what, they came from all walks of life. And some of them were not familiar with some of the finer points of the type of manners which are necessary in a naval officer's career later if he goes to any position of higher authority.

---

[*] A midshipman in his first year is called a plebe; second year, youngster or third classman; third year, second classman; fourth year, first classman.

But, in any event, the plebe year was intentionally—the word is not interesting—instructive year is a better term for it. And it was interesting from one point, that it was different from any other type of life I'd ever lived before.

John T. Mason: Was there some of that discipline in the Columbia Prep School?

Admiral McCain: There was not that kind of discipline. The kind of discipline in the Columbia Prep School was doing your homework and studying your lessons and when called upon to recite or work certain geometrical problems out, why, be prepared to do such and that sort. All of them interlocked, though, in some fashion or other.

But the plebe year at the Naval Academy, I put on about 20 pounds. And when it came time to go on my first cruise, youngster cruise, we used to call it, the third classmen, why, there was all the difference in the world between my physical being as of the preceding year and then. Another thing about it is, I had also had begun to accept and understand some of these things that were being done. I was known as a "ratey" plebe, and that's the plebe who does not conform always to the specific rules and regulations of the upperclassmen.

John T. Mason: [Laughter] A plebe with spirit.

Admiral McCain: Well, a plebe would come, and some of these upperclassmen would come up and make some of these statements to you, you know, and required you to do such things which only incited rebellion and mutiny in me, see. And although I did them, the attitude was there, see, and they didn't like that, see. But it was a fine institution.

Another thing that they injected thoroughly and completely in all of these young people there—and this same thing applies to West Point, and I'm sure that it applies to the Air Force Academy, too—and that is the highest sense of personal honor. And we've got to have that, because when a commander on the field of battle cannot rely on the accuracy and the forthrightness of the statements of his subordinates who may be commanding units in the field, as you can well see, on false information, he could well lose the battle.

And that's why this business of an honor system is so highly important, which has been under attack, I notice in the newspapers, at these schools, because—under the basis that it intrudes on a person's rights. Well, there's something a lot more important than that. But, again, I think that one of the most important aspects of going through a school like the Naval Academy is this one of training in a sense of highest personal honor in everything that you do. And I use this expression, rather than honesty, because honor implies across the entire spectrum of activities.

John T. Mason: It's a broader scope.

Admiral McCain: Yes, exactly right.

John T. Mason: Admiral Tommy Hart told me once upon a time that when he was there, the effort was made to develop leadership in men and also to turn them out as gentlemen.[*]

Admiral McCain: That's right.

John T. Mason: That's a fair estimate, is it not, of the intent of the training?

Admiral McCain: That's exactly right. There is a term which has slipped somewhat into disuse, which I always used till the moment I retired, and that is the statement "an officer and a gentleman." And those two imply everything that the highest sense of personal honor implies. And, incidentally, John Paul Jones spoke to the highest sense of personal honor, too, in an officer in the performance of his duty.[†] And you've got to have officers and gentlemen, because there are many times that an officer of high rank represents his

---

[*] Rear Admiral Thomas C. Hart, USN, was superintendent of the Naval Academy from May 1931 to June 1934. Dr. Mason interviewed Hart, who eventually retired as a four-star admiral, as part of the Columbia University oral history program.

[†] John Paul Jones (1747-1792) was the young country's first great naval officer and a hero of the Revolutionary War. He is credited with the following statement, though he probably did not express it in precisely these words: "It is by no means enough that an officer of the Navy should be a capable mariner. He must be that of course, but also a great deal more. He should be as well a gentleman of liberal education, refined manners, punctilious courtesy, and the nicest sense of personal honor."

country and represents his country with no other aid or factor to lean on. And he has got to do the job, and that's it.

John T. Mason: That's particularly true of the Navy, is it not, in past times, at least? The Navy got places where the Army didn't get.

Admiral McCain: Exactly. But in recent years, there has been an apparent change in that now.

John T. Mason: Yes.

Admiral McCain: I don't know how much it is, but you see more of the Army involved and more of the Air Force. I think that some of that will depend upon the instincts of the Commander in Chief, and that's what—when I speak of the Commander in Chief, I'm speaking of the President of the United States. It may be that he may want more naval than he does other types of advice or so forth and so on. But there's one thing I want to point out to you, and that is, despite space, despite air, despite land, the seas are going to have the predominating influence on the future of the United States, and you cannot avoid that. It's economic, it's political, it's military, and it's scientific. When I speak of scientific now, I'm speaking of such activities as oceanography and the science of the seas and all of that sort of thing. Now, when this concept will change—and I've always said this—is when there becomes some other method of sustaining heavy bodies in air rather than by airfoils. Just as soon as somebody comes along with an anti-gravity material, then I say to you this whole concept will change.

John T. Mason: Yes. Well, we'll wait for that.

Admiral McCain: Well, that may come, the way science moves, see, unless we destroy ourselves first.

John T. Mason: Going back to the Naval Academy, in retrospect, what is your estimate of the course of study when you were there, the caliber of it?

Admiral McCain: It was outstanding. We had more military instructors than we did civilian. And, you see, I was an instructor at the Naval Academy myself for two years, from '38 to '40. And there's one thing about an officer going back there as an instructor—I was more aware of many of the innermost aspects of the lives of these young midshipmen than were the professors themselves, and furthermore—

John T. Mason: Yes, because of the time span wasn't that great when you went back.

Admiral McCain: Well, that's right. Well, and another thing is that I knew. By that time, I had been out of the Naval Academy for seven years, and I'd had considerable submarine duty, and I knew by that time that many of the things that I had been taught and drilled into me were absolutely fundamental if we were going to maintain a Navy which was going to serve the country in good stead, which it did during World War II.

And, furthermore, when I was there as an instructor, there was a Captain J. H. Dessez, and I'll never forget that old captain.* He headed up electrical engineering and physics. I was an instructor in physics. And he said that from then on out, when I first got there, that the instructors would alternate with the professors on the lectures to these midshipmen. And I'm talking now not of the sections, now, of 15 to 20; I'm talking about a whole class of around maybe 300 or 400.

And it fell to my lot, being the junior one, to give the first lecture on physics. I learned as much as the midshipmen did from that first exercise. From then on, as self-confidence began to move in, why—and it served me in good stead the rest of my naval career, the fact that I had to do that, get up there and talk to these large number of people like this.

Because the trick—it's not a trick, but the fact of the matter is that when it comes to talking to large numbers of enlisted personnel—and in this last job I had, Army, Navy, Air Force, and Marine Corps—is not speaking technically to them, because we've got technical

---

* Captain John H. S. Dessez, USN.

experts all over the country. We've got them from MIT, we've got them from any school you can think of.* The thing that we do not have in great masses, and never will have, because it just so happens that the Lord fixed the world this way, and that is leaders, and that is, men that can sit up and talk to large numbers of enlisted personnel, in particular, or younger officers, or a combination of both, and inspire and get out of them what the country needs in its own defense.

I was invited to go back to the Naval Academy and make a graduation address, and I spent quite a bit of time on that address when I went back there. Jim Calvert, incidentally, was the superintendent at that time.† And I'll give you a copy of it if you ever want to see it.‡

John T. Mason: I would like to see it.

Admiral McCain: That thing meant a great deal to me to get up and—

John T. Mason: It incorporated a lot of your experience and philosophy.

Admiral McCain: It certainly did. And much to my astonishment, when I finished the speech, these kids got up, and they shouted and they hollered and they threw their hats in the air and so forth and so on. The point being that there was absolute approval of what I had to say by them, and it had done what I had wanted it to do, and that was it had an inspirational effect on them.

But the biggest and hardest job that any officer of any service has got is in the field of leadership. And, as I said before, you can always get a man who can tell you what the pounds per square inch of pressure is in a piston or what the stresses and strains of a hull, such as my friend Admiral Rickover can speak to of a submarine that dives and whatnot.§

---

* MIT—Massachusetts Institute of Technology.
† Rear Admiral/Vice Admiral James F. Calvert, USN, served as superintendent of the Naval Academy from July 1968 to June 1972.
‡ A copy of the address, which Admiral McCain delivered on 3 June 1970, is included as an appendix in this volume.
§ Hyman G. Rickover was considered the father of the nuclear Navy. He ran the U.S. Navy's nuclear-power program for many years, from 1948 until he eventually left active duty in 1982 with the rank of four-star admiral on the retired list. Rickover Hall at the Naval Academy is named in his honor.

But the business of leadership is another matter entirely. And that is, again, one of the most difficult subjects that there is, and it's the most difficult to inspire in people subordinate to you—a desire to do a better job.

John T. Mason: At the academy, it's a subtle sort of thing, isn't it?

Admiral McCain: Yes, very subtle. You can't put it in mathematical terms.

John T. Mason: But it depends upon the personnel, the teaching staff, I would think, in great measure.

Admiral McCain: Of course, when a young ensign comes out of the Naval Academy, it's going to take him a long time. He's got to continually and constantly work on this himself, within himself. And I believe in God. And I believe that a higher power has something to do with this too. You get into more formidable aspects of leadership, and there are very few real leaders that I've ever had contact with in my life in both civilian and military. The standard of leadership of young officers coming out of the Naval Academy is very high as a group, but when it comes to the type of leadership I'm talking to you about that we need, when a man is much further along and has larger groups and doesn't have the full advantage of personal contact continuing constantly with those he's trying to lead, that gets into a very difficult arrangement.

John T. Mason: Since you touch on the subject of your belief in God, in retrospect, what value was the chapel in the life of the Naval Academy?

Admiral McCain: It was a very, very fine and outstanding influence, and I was very much disturbed when I found out the chapel had been stopped at the Naval Academy.

John T. Mason: The compulsory attendance.

Admiral McCain: Yes, that's right, what they call compulsory attendance. Now, they made us go, and it may have been sometimes we marched to chapel with less than the highest of religious thoughts and so forth. Nevertheless, there came a time in the lives of every one of the midshipmen that I knew around my time when they knew where to turn to when they had to rely on God. And for a man who goes into battle, believe me, there comes a time when he relies on a higher power to help him through certain aspects of whatever the battle may be, and so forth. And I feel very strongly on this subject. And I think you'll find anybody who's ever been subject to a situation of life and death, that he feels very strongly on the business of at least exposing these young people to chapel.

Now, all this elimination of chapel fits right in with this general liberal, left-wing atmosphere which is pervading the country anyway, see, which is another point that's bad.

John T. Mason: What about your athletic activities while you were at the academy?

Admiral McCain: I was too damn little.

John T. Mason: You could have gone out for bantam-weight things.

Admiral McCain: Yeah, I know, but you see, when I graduated, it seems to me I weighed 120, but most of the time, I weighed about 110 or someplace in there. And in order to box in the bantam weight, you had to weigh, I think it was 112 or something like that—I've forgotten what it was—though I did box. And I did learn how to jump rope, and I jump rope now every morning, as a matter of exercise, because it's a stupid exercise and it makes you concentrate on what you're doing. And it's better than jogging, because when you jump rope, if your feet aren't in the air at the same time the rope hits the ground, you don't jump rope. With jogging, all you've got to do is put one foot in front of the other, you see.

John T. Mason: Did you go in for tennis?

Admiral McCain: Yep, I played tennis and I played—for several years I played tennis. Then my father misled me by telling me I ought to take up golf, because he said you get to know the people you're playing with better and this sort of thing, which is right. But after the war, I went back into tennis again, and I've been playing tennis ever since. You can play tennis anyplace. I've played it out in the Far East in every tennis court they've got, all the way from Japan and Korea right on down to Australia and New Zealand.

John T. Mason: Tell me about the summer cruises at the academy and their influence on you in the development of your naval career.

Admiral McCain: Well, the summer cruises were not always the kind of cruises that were the best for midshipmen, in this sense—that they were limited in the geographical scope of the cruise itself. The first summer cruise that I took as a youngster, we just went up and down the East Coast. And we went into New York, and we went into Norfolk, and we went into Newport. I forget that place up there in Maine we went to. And this sort of thing.

John T. Mason: That wasn't anything new for you.

Admiral McCain: No. And the one thing that did come out of the cruise, however—in those days, we all slept in hammocks. And they used to turn out all hands. We never called it reveille, I mean, the days I was in the Navy. They used to turn all hands out at around 5:30 in the morning. And they made you put seven lashings on the hammock, and then when you took it to the hammock nettings, where the hammocks were stored, there was a tough boatswain's mate standing there with a hoop about that big. And if your hammock wouldn't fit through that with the lashings on it, you had to go back and relash the hammock so it did. And then, of course, right after that, they served coffee. That's where I got in this bad habit of drinking so damn much coffee all the time. Then, after that, we got up there and we scrubbed decks. And when we got through with scrubbing decks, we had breakfast.

John T. Mason: You had a real appetite by that time.

Admiral McCain: Yeah. And then after breakfast, why, we got out on the ship's work of the day, or, for midshipmen, they used to have some instruction courses for us, such things as in engineering and also in gunnery and ordnance and this sort of thing.

John T. Mason: Were these instructors from the academy who were on board?

Admiral McCain: Yes, most of them were.

John T. Mason: This was on a battleship?

Admiral McCain: This was on the battleship, that's right. And the big thing that came out of the battleship was not so much that, but the fact that you learned as a young midshipman that when you're living aboard ship, it's an entirely different life than living ashore. And don't ever let anybody delude you on that one, incidentally. And it doesn't make any difference whether the ship's tied up alongside the dock or whether it's at sea; it's a world unto itself.

Furthermore, a battleship, carrier, destroyer, submarine, you've got to maintain a high level of discipline, because when men live that close together, they have to conform with the rules and regulations. Otherwise, somebody—his life is intruded upon in a fashion which is beyond the scope of the lesson, so to speak.

But the big thing we got out of those cruises—the first class cruise, we went to Cherbourg, and we went to Europe and places like that and enjoyed that thoroughly too. But, incidentally, the only reason we took that East Coast cruise in my youngster cruise is because the United States was going through another economic crisis, in which we were not spending too much money on anything, so to speak.

But, in any event, the big thing that came out of both cruises was how to live aboard ship, which is different than living ashore, and it's a lot different than living aboard one of these nice, beautiful cruise ships that go to Bermuda and this sort of thing—where you're handed an instrument that can, if the circumstances required, deal out death and destruction to a potential enemy. There was a lot of difference between the life and so forth.

And every time you read in the newspapers, incidentally—for example, we've had trouble, as you know, with the racial problem in the United States Navy. You want to always keep in mind, regardless of what, that a ship is something all by itself, regardless of anything else that may happen, and it's separate from the rest of the world. Within that hull, it's a world unto itself, and it has to be handled as a world unto itself.

I objected strenuously to Admiral Zumwalt's let-down in the standards of personal appearance and other matters, and with that went a let-down in the standards in the discipline, the standards of the upkeep of machinery and this sort of thing.[*] And it hurt the Navy considerably, that period of time. And how long it's going to take to get a Navy back to where you've got the standards of discipline that we need in a Navy, I don't know.

John T. Mason: Can it be achieved? Can we go back and undo some of the things that were done?

Admiral McCain: Yes, they're being done now. This Admiral Holloway is an outstanding Chief of Naval Operations.[†] And he's more than aware of these difficulties that you and I are talking about, but—as with a lot of things in life—you just don't do it overnight. You just can't turn a back flip and have the whole thing change, see.

But aboard these various ships that I took midshipman cruises on, again, I want to go back to this business of moral discipline and a sense of honor. This is the thing that was instilled from the time that I was a plebe at the Naval Academy until I got to the point where I was a responsible officer myself and was trying to do the same thing down the line. And that's what the Naval Academy, West Point, and the Air Force Academy—one of their greatest responsibilities is graduating young officers from those schools that have this personal sense of honor.

John T. Mason: It becomes second nature in their lives.

---

[*] Admiral Elmo R. Zumwalt, Jr., USN, served as Chief of Naval Operations from 1 July 1970 to 29 June 1974. During his tenure he made a great many dramatic innovations that attempted to deal with such issues as enlisted rights and privileges, equal opportunity, and Navy families. Junior personnel generally viewed the changes much more favorably than did their seniors.
[†] Admiral James L. Holloway III, USN, served as Chief of Naval Operations from 29 June 1974 to 1 July 1978. He was the incumbent at the time of this interview.

Admiral McCain: Yes.

John T. Mason: Well now, you had a head start on this, of course, and I suppose all young men—

Admiral McCain: What do you mean, a head start?

John T. Mason: In that you came from a Navy family where this tradition was inculcated. Some of these boys came from the prairies of the Middle West and didn't have this as their background.

Admiral McCain: No, I don't say that. My grandfather had a plantation in Mississippi; my father came from that. I think that there are certain groups of people in the country, or families, or whatever you want to call them, that live by these principles anyway. You and I know bums and crooks and thieves when we went to school, regardless of what family they came from. And they can come from some of the so-called highest level families of the land, if you want to call them that too.

But the big thing at the Naval Academy—and I didn't have any head start with these people on this sort of thing—but the big point was that I had been taught to be honest as a boy myself. And I will say that 99 and 44/100% of my classmates were that way too. Isn't that what Ivory soap's supposed to be—99 and 44/100% pure? And there were a couple that were thrown out because of gouging, cheating—as it's known in public life—and so forth. But I don't subscribe to this head start thing at all.

I think that there were a number of people who went to the school that were brought up the same way that I was, regardless of what. Now, when it comes to having seen a ship, maybe I had a head start there. But I certainly didn't have a head start when we all moved aboard that ship that morning at 6:00 o'clock with our hammocks, because I didn't have the slightest idea what I was getting into. I'd never been on a ship in my life to live that way. In fact, I don't ever remember being on a ship and living on one before I went to the Naval Academy.

Again, we have got to have an officer corps that will go forth and fight for this country and die when the time comes and will lead the people to do it. And when I was commander in chief out there, I made it a point to go out at least once a month to South Vietnam and sometimes more often, and always Christmas.[*] I was up at the DMZ area, and I would sit down with these soldiers and talk to them and open myself up to any questions that they wanted to ask, and anything that they wanted to say.[†] And I want to tell you that the modern American youth, by and large, is a very fine young fellow.

One Christmas, I went up to the DMZ. There were 30 soldiers sitting in this little area we were in, and the sergeant gave to me a bunch of papers that had been dropped on the U.S. lines by balloons that the North Vietnamese used to release. And in these papers were columns by Jack Anderson and Drew Pearson, in those days, and statements by certain leaders back here in the country, that do anything but instill patriotic compliance with the U.S. flag and this sort of thing.[‡] This sergeant said, "What do you think of that, Admiral?"

I said, "Sergeant, you know as well as I do that the primary purpose of your presence here and my presence as your commanding officer is to make sure that the United States is so secure that damn fools can make such damn fool statements as you've shown me here, and do this in a certain measure of safety." And I feel very strongly on that subject.

I notice now, incidentally, in all the papers, there's a great to-do about—not all the papers but some of them—about the fact that we should never have been in Vietnam in the first place. Well, I just want to tell you that the Communist is about to win the battle out there, and he's going to take over all of that Southeast Asian peninsula, and that just means another great segment.[§]

I had a man tell me the other day, of some standing in our own government—he says, "Why, who cares about Southeast Asia? That's not a very important area."

---

[*] Admiral McCain served as Commander in Chief Pacific from 31 July 1968 to 1 September 1972.
[†] DMZ—the demilitarized zone that divided North Vietnam from South Vietnam.
[‡] Andrew Pearson was a muckraking syndicated newspaper columnist, the predecessor of Jack Anderson.
[§] On 29-30 April 1975, just a few months after this interview with Admiral McCain, North Vietnamese overran Saigon, the capital of South Vietnam. U.S. Navy and Marine Corps helicopters evacuated almost 9,000 people. Included were 1,373 Americans, 6,422 of other nationalities, plus 989 Marines inserted to cover the operation. Graham Martin, U.S. ambassador to South Vietnam, was among the last to leave from the rooftop of the American embassy.

Well, then who cares about India? Who cares about the Middle East? Who cares about anything? All these areas, see. And when Southeast Asia is finally taken over again, which there is a great danger of this happening, it won't be the first time that that peninsula, I might add, has been occupied by the Red Chinese. They're moving more to prominence out there now, and they're just beginning to stir.

But, going back to the Naval Academy, all the training that I had at the Naval Academy and all of the attitudes that were injected into me was one of them: if it's necessary, die for your country. This sounds hard-boiled, it sounds anything, but we have got to have young men who will go forth and die for their country. And, of course, an outstanding example of this is my son, Johnny, who, thank God almighty, he came out of it alive. He was a POW for five and a half years.[*]

John T. Mason: What an ordeal.

Admiral McCain: Sure was. I just got through, as I think I told you, spending five days with him down there in Jacksonville.

John T. Mason: Well, sir, were there any exciting events during your academy career that you want to recall? Did you get in any hot water?

Admiral McCain: Yes, I got into hot water. I got into such hot water on—I'm trying to think back now. I know at one time that there was some question about whether I was going to graduate from the school. See, for our first class year, if you exceeded 150 demerits—now, these demerits could come from anything from a bed that wasn't properly made up to anything of a much higher order, see, and us boys used to do a thing called "frenching out," which is not all, by a long shot.[†]

And I got caught in one of these little affairs, and the battalion commander, who was an actual commander in the Navy, got me down and he said, "If we get one more

---

[*] Lieutenant Commander John S. McCain III, USN, a naval aviator, was a prisoner in North Vietnam from 1967 to 1973. He retired as a captain in 1981 and was subsequently elected to the House of Representatives in 1982 and the U.S. Senate in 1986.
[†] "French out" is midshipman slang for leaving the Naval Academy without authorization.

demerit on you, McCain, we're either going to turn you back into the next class, or you'll be dropped from the muster roll." He said, "I can't tell you which will happen, but you can rest assured one of the two will." So from then on out, for the next three months, I shined my shoes and everything else and did everything right. When it came time for me to graduate, I took my diploma, and I went. I think that was the closest call I had.

We used to go out in town to a house there that was run by God knows who—I don't know. And it wasn't a whorehouse, but we used to go out there and drink beer. And this was the days of Prohibition, if you will recall.[*]

John T. Mason: So that was a double demerit.

Admiral McCain: Yes. But we could get the beer there. This old gal that ran the house, why, she was nice as she could be to all of us midshipmen. I've often wondered why she never got caught at that, come to think of it, but she never did.

I think another time at the Naval Academy, youngster year, I loafed through the first month of the second semester, and then had to spend the rest of that time studying to pull myself satisfactory in all of my marks and so forth and so on and whatnot. I don't know whether, in retrospect, I wasted my time on something like that or not, but I'll tell you one thing, you get to know people that you don't ordinarily know if you're one of the good boys, see. And sometimes the world's not always made up of all the good boys, either, by a long shot.

John T. Mason: What did you do with your leave, your Christmas leave? Your family was near at hand.

Admiral McCain: Well, the first Christmas leave, my family was out on the West Coast because my father was on the New Mexico, and so I spent with my roommate, a young

---

[*] The 18th Amendment to the Constitution was ratified in 1919 and went into effect in 1920, prohibiting the consumption of alcoholic beverages in the United States. The Volstead Act, enacted by Congress in 1919, spelled out the penalties for violations. In December 1933 the ratification of the 21st Amendment to the Constitution repealed the 18th Amendment and thus ended national prohibition.

fellow named Eddie Seidel.* I wonder what happened to Eddie? He lived out here in Takoma Park.† But his family were nice enough to take me in for that Christmas leave period out there. The next two Christmas leave periods, however, or three, rather, were spent right here in Washington because my family was here. And that's when they lived up here on 20th Street.

John T. Mason: You must have been very popular with Washington girls, were you?

Admiral McCain: Well, no. I was not—not the right kind. [Laughter] In those days, of course, the big thing—and I don't know whether it still is or not because I haven't checked on it since—but in those days were the debutante parties, you know. Most of them used to take place right around Christmas on purpose, because not only the Naval Academy and West Point, but all the colleges were off on vacation too. I went to a number of those.

John T. Mason: You were on Mrs. Egner's list, I guess.

Admiral McCain: I don't know. I was on somebody's list. But I don't regret it. I may have wasted time; I doubt it, in one respect, but I enjoyed thoroughly my life on the face of this earth. I can't say I enjoyed the Naval Academy all the time, because it placed too many restrictions on my own personal ideas of what I wanted to do, and things of that sort. The Naval Academy was not an easy school in those days. They were pretty rough on midshipmen, and they should be.

Another thing is that they're getting a free education off the government. That's another point I feel very strongly about in these schools.

John T. Mason: What percentage of the lads stayed in the Navy and were given commissions?

---

* Midshipman Harry Edward Seidel, Jr., USN. Seidel graduated from the Naval Academy in the class of 1931, eventually retired as a captain in 1948, and died in 1983.
† Takoma Park, Maryland, is a suburb of Washington, D.C.

Admiral McCain: I don't know. I can find out. I'd have to check that. It was a good percentage, I'll tell you that.

John T. Mason: Of course, you came out in the time of Depression too.*

Admiral McCain: That's right, and another thing was, don't forget, the Navy was small. The armed forces were small. And the very fact that you had a uniform, you enjoyed a certain amount of respect right on that basis. A man in uniform in those days could go in and get a check cashed anyplace without having to show everything from his birth certificate to all the rest of the identification that goes with it.

John T. Mason: This is witness to the man of honor, isn't it?

Admiral McCain: That's right. It was different in that respect; there isn't any question about it. The world is just changing. The thing about the United States itself, and the reason that I'm going back into public speaking again, is because the United States itself is not aware of the terrific danger of what Russia's doing and that Red China is just beginning to move, and some of these other aspects. Soviet Russia is building a tremendous navy, and she is just beginning to move in this area.

Another thing about a lot of naval officers, they don't understand Mahan.† Mahan talked to sea power from the standpoint of naval power, economic power, scientific exploration of the ocean depths. And, of course, one of his big points was the business of the merchant marine and fishing industry. And it's a very remarkable book he wrote. And Gorshkov, in some respects, has written a book which is comparable to what—and I hate to say this about Russians, because I don't have any sympathy for them whatsoever—but

---

* Following the crash of the New York Stock Exchange in late October 1929, the United States was plunged into the Great Depression, from which it did not recover until the nation geared up for World War II at the beginning of the 1940s. The Depression was marked by high unemployment and many business failures.

† Alfred Thayer Mahan (1840-1914) was the United States's most influential naval historian and philosopher. His lectures at the Naval War College led to his greatest work, The Influence of Sea Power upon History, 1660-1783, published in 1890. His writings stimulated the growth of a large Navy and the nation's overseas expansion. As a senior officer, McCain gave countless speeches on the subject of sea power.

which is some respects comparable to what Mahan had to say.* I'm not so damn sure that Gorshkov may not have—

John T. Mason: Plagiarized?

Admiral McCain: Yes. Not directly by direct quote, but certainly by having studied the book himself.

John T. Mason: Well, if it's truth, it would apply to us and to the Russians as well, in terms of naval parlance.

Admiral McCain: Well, you see, one of the great empires of the world was the British Empire, and for someplace in the neighborhood of two centuries there was a relative measure of peace.

John T. Mason: Admiral, when you were at the Naval Academy as a midshipman, what in the program encouraged young men to speak and to write? What was done to train them in these areas?

Admiral McCain: There was not enough done, but, nevertheless, an effort was made. And periodically—and I've forgotten how often—particularly first class year, we used to have a formal dinner. It was stag, and this would be presided over by a professor from English, History and Government, which we were required—each one at his particular time—to make an after-dinner speech. That was one. The second one, of course, was that we were also required to make certain addresses in the class itself at appropriate times on appropriate subjects when it would arise. But there wasn't nearly enough of it done. And there ought to be a lot more. I don't know how they're doing down there now about this thing, but there ought to be a lot of that.

---

* Admiral of the Fleet of the Soviet Union S. G. Gorshkov served as Commander in Chief of the Soviet Navy from January 1956 to December 1985. He expressed his views in a series of articles on Navies in War and in Peace. They appeared in the book Red Star Rising at Sea, published in 1974 by the Naval Institute Press.

John T. Mason: And in the area of writing, what experience did you get?

Admiral McCain: Well, again, in writing, they would require us to write certain theses when we were second and first classmen. I know first class for a fact, and I think we did the same thing second class too. But that was about the limit of this sort of a thing. And this was one of the areas which the Naval Academy—and I don't know, maybe it's greatly improved in this area, because I haven't looked at their curriculum, and I'm unfamiliar with what they require these young men to do now.

But you have put your finger on a highly important aspect of life, because later there comes a time in which they've got to be able to, first, talk to bluejackets and younger officers, and next they've got to be back here in the arena in Washington, D.C., to argue the case in the Pentagon building before various groups. Then, of course, one of the ultimate areas is appearing before these congressional committees. And I was in congressional liaison for three years, which was another great asset in my career. And I headed up public information for a year and a half or two, which helped greatly in all these areas. Writing, as you well know, is the toughest job that there is in the world, regardless of what.

John T. Mason: It just takes practice.

When you graduated, what kind of a career was before you?

Admiral McCain: Well, when I first graduated, in those days, you had to go to sea for two years as a junior officer either in a battleship or a carrier. Then at the end of that two years, you had the choice, if you could pass the physical exam, of going to Pensacola for flight training or to the submarine school at New London, Connecticut. And I could not pass the physical exam for flight training because—

John T. Mason: Were you intrigued with the idea?

Admiral McCain: Oh, yeah, I'd have liked to have gone to Pensacola, but I had a rapid pulse, and they had in those days a thing called the Schneider heart test, where they took your blood pressure—sitting, and lying down, every other damn way, and a few other things, and your pulse and so forth.

John T. Mason: After jumping the rope too.

Admiral McCain: So I finally put in for the submarine school. And they had an equally tough examination, but it wasn't along quite the same lines. They were more interested up there in how the body itself would take pressures and this sort of thing, see. And so I went into submarines in 1933 and was in submarines until well after World War II.

John T. Mason: Tell me about your experience on the battleship first.* What did you add to your knowledge?

Admiral McCain: It added a tremendous amount to my knowledge. I was very fortunate, in that they sent me in as a communication watch officer first. Now, that sounds like just an ordinary job, but when you do it properly and become interested in what you're doing, there was a tremendous amount of information that passed through my hands to the captain of the ship and vice versa. And it was a tremendous amount of classified information on the world situation and things of that sort, and gave me an opportunity to also learn the communication procedures of the fleet at that time—not from a technical viewpoint, because I was not a technician in any sense, but I've always been thankful that I had that opportunity. I think that lasted about the first year I was aboard, or the first eight or nine months.

John T. Mason: Did you have an inspiring set of officers on board?

Admiral McCain: Yes, after a fashion. The Navy at that time had a number of officers left over from World War I who were serving their time, but the officer that I served with was

---

* From 1931 to 1933, as an ensign, McCain served on board the USS Oklahoma (BB-37), which had been commissioned 2 May 1916. She had a standard displacement of 27,500 tons, was 583 feet long, and 95 feet in the beam. Her top speed was 20.5 knots. Her main battery comprised ten 14-inch guns. She later capsized at her berth during the Japanese attack on Pearl Harbor in December 1941.

the communication officer, a man named Bill Ammon, was outstanding in every respect.[*] I don't know what ever happened to him.[†] You can imagine the communication department you would have to have one of the better.

Then I went from there to the fourth division, which made me a junior officer in the turret back there, but also they made me the catapult officer. Now, that was outstanding training, to say the least. And the first time I launched an aviator off that catapult, there was a mistake in the signals, and, as he said later, he was sitting on the catapult with his arm extended one minute, and the next minute he found himself 3,000 feet in the air flying around with the rest of the boys, see. And that was one time I was really afraid that they were going to pull me out of that, but they didn't, God bless them, and they let me in it. And from then on out, why, it went fine. That begat a basic knowledge of ordnance and so forth.

And it was about that time, also, that they began to put in requests that we young officers go to these various other branches such as submarines, such as aviation.

John T. Mason: Did you demonstrate early on a very great interest in ordnance as such?

Admiral McCain: No. I did to some degree, but when I went into the Navy, to be in ordnance, really, you had to go to postgraduate schools after six years and take the ordnance course, one. Two, to be in ordnance, you had to stand way at the top of your class. The ordnance people, along with the people in naval construction, were very particular about the intellectual level of the people they took. I never equaled either one of these outfits, but I was interested in ordnance from one standpoint, and that is what you could do with it, of course, if you had to. But it never gave me any feeling because I couldn't get into the postgraduate school on any of these courses that I was left out.[‡]

And, as a matter of fact, when it came time to go to PG School, the United States Navy, in its ultimate wisdom, sent me down there to the Naval Academy as an instructor, rather than going down to take the general line course at the PG School. And I've always

---

[*] Lieutenant William B. Ammon, USN.
[†] Ammon eventually retired as a rear admiral; he died in 1959.
[‡] Originally established at Annapolis, Maryland, on 9 June 1909, the Naval Postgraduate School was later moved to the grounds of the former Hotel Del Monte in Monterey, California, in June 1951.

been thankful to the Navy for making such a colossal blunder, because I got a lot more out of getting up there every day on my feet in front of those midshipmen and instructing and talking and explaining "force equals mass times acceleration" and all the rest of these things than I would ever have gotten if I'd gone to that Postgraduate School over there, because I'm not a good student, anyway, and never have been, particularly. It would have annoyed me no end to go up there to some instructor at the Postgraduate School, and when I felt that I knew more than him than him trying to tell me what should be done in a certain area, see. But that was the real thing.

And then, of course, by the time I'd gone to instruction at the Naval Academy down there, I was already in submarines. I had been in submarines then for four years, I guess it was. And the next big trick was to get back into submarines, because they were selective in submarines like they were not in any other branch of the Navy. And, much to my pleased astonishment, I got selected to go back into submarines again, see.

So going there as an instructor did not hurt. It brought out sharply one point, and that is, if an officer goes into a job, he can make anything out of it he wants to. He can make it an outstanding job of the highest repute, or he can go in there with an attitude which is no good, and he'll lose out every time.

John T. Mason: How influential was your father in helping you shape your career?

Admiral McCain: He wasn't—nothing, except the business of the fact that I had learned from him the importance of command. It doesn't make any difference where you go; you've got to command.

John T. Mason: Well, I was thinking when you were on the battleship and thinking about going to submarine school, did you consult him? What was his advice?

Admiral McCain: Yes, I said that to him. He said, "Yes, fine, go right ahead, son." He said, "The only thing I say to you is to make a good job out of it." And that was it. I don't think that my father cared too much whether I went into naval air or submarines, as long as I made a good job out of the thing, see. That was his point.

John T. Mason: So the battleship experience was a very good one indeed. Did some of your classmates serve with you on board?

Admiral McCain: Oh, yes. In the battleships of those days, we used to have a junior officers' mess, in which there were about, oh, I'd say, 20-25 junior officers there, of which I would say someplace in the neighborhood of 12 of them were classmates of mine. We enjoyed ourselves thoroughly. It was a wonderful life to lead after being thrown out of the Naval Academy. My God!

John T. Mason: Was this in the Pacific or Atlantic?

Admiral McCain: It's in the Pacific. All of a sudden we'd get into a place where we got messboys to shine our shoes and all the rest of this sort of thing that we'd been doing for four years. I can't tell you what a change in life it was. All you had to do was to push a button, and a messboy would bring you a cup of coffee, see, and this sort of thing. It was a marvelous life.

John T. Mason: Were there any interesting maneuvers on which you went? Admiral Reeves was in command of the fleet, was he not?[*]

Admiral McCain: I think so. I didn't—yeah, he was. And there were no interesting maneuvers. They were all standard maneuvers out there in the Pacific. There was nothing of any international impact out there in that area at that time or anything of that sort.

John T. Mason: The Navy was somewhat curbed anyway, was it not, because of the Depression and the lack of funds?

---

[*] Admiral Joseph M. Reeves, USN, served as Commander in Chief U.S. Fleet from 15 June 1934 to 24 June 1936.

Admiral McCain: Yes. We couldn't make extended cruises, really, for any length of time. I remember one cruise out to Honolulu and back, and I remember that we made another cruise up to Seattle. And then another time, the Oklahoma went up there and we went into overhaul in the Bremerton Navy Yard, which, of course, doesn't fit into the category of cruises. But they ought to take these young people on cruises, because there's something to seeing, as against reading, writing, being talked to about. And if you go to some of these places, many times it will either affirm or disavow or it will give you new lines of thought, and so forth, if you go on this sort of thing with something serious as a purpose.

John T. Mason: What sort of facilities did we have at Pearl Harbor when you went out there on the Oklahoma?

Admiral McCain: Well, in the first place, when we went out there, they had these mooring points for all these battleships that were caught by the Japanese on December 7 of 1941. But it was not a big and complete naval organization out there, by a long shot. Four or five years later—when I went out there about four years later, I guess it was, when I went out there on the S-45, a submarine, it was an entirely different setup.* It had begun to grow and develop then.

John T. Mason: But there was in '31-'32, there was some kind of submarine base, was there not?

Admiral McCain: There was a submarine base there, very definitely so. But for taking care of a whole fleet, it did not have the capacity that it did have four years later, because they were working on it then. There were funds that were going into this thing at that time, see, despite the fact that the country was just getting over a Depression and whatnot.

---

* USS S-45 (SS-156) was commissioned on 31 March 1925. She was 225 feet long, 21 feet in the beam, displaced 850 tons surfaced and 1,126 tons submerged. She was armed with four 21-inch torpedo tubes and had a top speed of 14.5 knots surfaced and 11 knots submerged. She was the first boat in which McCain served after completing Submarine School in December 1933.

John S. McCain, Jr. (1/6/75) – Page 32

John T. Mason: Well, sir, shall we go back to New London now to the submarine school, after you'd made your decision to go there? How many classmates went with you?

Admiral McCain: In the whole class up there, there were someplace in the neighborhood of 30, of which I would say maybe about 10 or 12 were classmates out of the Naval Academy. And these classes ranged all the way from '28, '29, '30, and '31, the four classes, if I remember right, when I went up there. And the course at the submarine school was good.

John T. Mason: And rigorous, too, was it not?

Admiral McCain: Yes. And this was the result, as you well know, of the S-51 going down and things of this sort.* Furthermore, the introduction of the Momsen lung, submarine lung, had just occurred.† And they had one of these 110-foot diving tanks up there, which was nothing but a tank of water 110 feet high.

And one of the tests they made us go through was to go into a compartment comparable to that of a forward torpedo room of a submarine of that day, an S-class submarine. They would flood the compartment so that there was a capsule of air for you to breathe in at the top. They would then pass out these lungs—this Momsen lung I was telling you about, nothing but a rubber sack that you hung in front of you and breathed into. And it had a chemical in it, I've forgotten which, which purified the air. And then they would open the hatch and release a buoy, which took a line to the top of this thing. And then we would come up, hanging onto that line, just slow our way up. The line had a certain number of knots on it that. At each knot you were supposed to stop and take a certain number of breaths. This was to keep you from getting into bends, divers' bends.

---

* On the night of 25 September 1925, the USS S-51 (SS-162) was rammed and sunk off Block Island, New York, by the merchant steamer City of Rome. Of the 36 men on board the submarine, only three survived. For a compelling account by the principal salvage officer, see Edward Ellsberg, On the Bottom (New York: Literary Guild of America, Inc., 1929).
† Invented by submariner Charles B. Momsen, the Momsen lung was a breathing apparatus to be used when ascending from a damaged submarine to the surface. It did not have its own air supply but used the air already in a man's lungs.

And later they went to what was known as the continuous-ascent procedure, in which you came out of the forward torpedo room of this submarine compartment at the bottom of this tank and put your hands and feet on this line and kept yourself from bouncing to the surface by coming up at a constant rate without stopping anyplace. And this continuous-ascent method is the method by which from then on out we began to teach all submariners to do business, in the event they ever had to make an escape from a submarine.

John T. Mason: Like climbing the rungs of a ladder, coming up?

Admiral McCain: Yes, but as I say, with continuous ascent, all you did was to hang onto the line with your hands and feet and allowed yourself, without stopping anyplace, to continually come on up, see. As you came up, the pressure inside the body was greater than the pressure at the surface of the water, so as you started up, you gained more positive buoyancy as the air expanded. Well, the big trick was to make sure that as you exhaled, that you did it at a sufficient rate and you made this continuous ascent at a sufficient rate so that the body did not accumulate any pockets of high-pressure air, which in turn would cause the bends.

And this is the manner in which we did it after that. Each year they used to make submariners go through this training in the diving tank. They had a diving tank out at Pearl Harbor, I might add, for the same purpose. I think they had one in San Diego—I'm not sure—but I know they had it in New London and Pearl Harbor.

But the submarine school itself had some very fine lieutenants as instructors up there, and they knew their business. They had been specially selected for this. And the second point was that submarines itself had become a highly selective business, because I think of the 30 of us that went to the school were selectees out of something like maybe 150 who had put in for it.

John T. Mason: So it was a very dangerous business, was it not?

Admiral McCain: Well, you might say it was dangerous, but, no, I don't think submarines are real dangerous until you get into a good war with these damn things. But not any more dangerous than flying a plane.

John T. Mason: You used the S class primarily.

Admiral McCain: Yes. In those days, the S class. The fleet-type submarine that we used in World War II, in 1933 or thereabouts, was just coming into existence.[*] The Electric Boat Company of Groton, Connecticut, right below the submarine base at New London, was just beginning to turn out its first submarines, and also they built this type of submarine up there at Portsmouth, New Hampshire, and they also built them out there at Mare Island, California. And that was the submarine that did so much damage to the Japanese.

And it was diesel-electric, which the present type submarine with nuclear power far exceeds in value anything that I ever knew in submarines. You can stay submerged forever on those things, relatively speaking, maybe a month, two months, something like that, see. They have air purification apparatus and all this other sort of thing.

John T. Mason: The S class was inspired by Simon Lake, was it not?

Admiral McCain: The submarine as a whole was inspired by him.[†] I say the S class was developed, but from the A-class submarine, which may have been what Simon Lake put out. I don't know. The A class was a small submarine which had a crew, I guess, of about ten or something like that. Now, the S-45 had a crew of someplace in the neighborhood of 39. Then, when I went to the Skipjack, the Gunnel, and the Dentuda, which were the fleet type that did the job during the war, the crew on those submarines ran around 50 or 60.

---

[*] USS Cachalot (SS-170), the name ship of her class, was commissioned 1 December 1933. She had a displacement of 1,110 tons on the surface and 1,650 tons submerged. She was 272 feet long, 25 feet in the beam, and had a draft of 13 feet. Her top speed was 17 knots surfaced and 8 knots submerged. She was armed with six 21-inch torpedo tubes and a 3-inch deck gun. Further refinements were still needed in subsequent classes, but the Cachalot resembled the highly successful fleet boats of World War II.

[†] Simon Lake (1866-1945) was a mechanical engineer and naval architect. He invented the even-keel-type submarine and in 1897 built the Argonaut, which was the first submarine to operate successfully in the open sea. The submarine tender Simon Lake (AS-33) was named in his honor.

And they were good submarines. Boy, they were damn good. And they came along just in time to serve the purpose that was necessary for the needs of this country in the war with Japan.

But, in any event, that course at New London . . .

John T. Mason: How long was that course?

Admiral McCain: . . . only lasted six months. And then we were ordered to submarines from there, and I went to the S-45 out in Honolulu. I was aboard the S-45 until I was ordered back to the Naval Academy as an instructor. And from the Naval Academy as an instructor, I went to a new fleet-type submarine, the Skipjack, as the executive officer.*

John T. Mason: Tell me first about the S-45, her operations out of Pearl.

Admiral McCain: They were easy, I mean, compared with what we had to do with submarines later. We used to take those submarines, diesel-electric, the diesel-engine type—the diesel engines were a much more antiquated type than the diesel engines we had in the Skipjack.

John T. Mason: They were first developed in Germany, were they not, the diesel?

Admiral McCain: I suppose. I don't think they came from Germany. I don't know where these engines came from. I think that Germany had gone beyond us at that stage, see. I'm not sure whether they had or not. Diesel engines were developed in Germany, but I don't think that has anything to do with what I'm saying to you now, because these were engines, I think, actually developed up there at the Electric Boat Company in Groton, Connecticut. They were a crude engine, and when you came to the type of engine we had later in

---

* USS Skipjack (SS-184) was a Gato-class submarine commissioned 30 June 1938. She had a displacement of 1,449 tons on the surface and 2,198 tons submerged. She was 308 feet long, 26 feet in the beam, and had a draft of 14 feet. Her top speed was 21 knots surfaced and 9 knots submerged. She was armed with eight 21-inch torpedo tubes and a 3-inch deck gun.

submarines, and we used to go out and operate on these engines, submerge and make torpedo approaches and then come back in.

Most of the time, we were never out even overnight on these old S-boats. They were rough to travel in, temperatures around 110 degrees Fahrenheit all the time, the humidity was high. And you had to be young to be in it; you had to love it to do it right, see.

But when it came to the fleet-type submarine that did the job during World War II, we had dehumidifiers, the air purifiers. The air purifiers weren't much, but the dehumidifiers did plenty. They took the moisture out of the air, which made it that much easier to live aboard. And, furthermore, where this submarine, the S-boats, can only make nine or ten knots on the surface, a submarine like the Skipjack or the Gunnel or the Dentuda, we could make someplace in the neighborhood of 18 or 19 knots on the surface under diesel power.

Now, submerged, all these submarines were limited to a maximum speed of around eight or nine knots, which meant that your battery power was gone within an hour, so when we were actually operating submerged, we had to travel around speeds of maybe five knots, four knots, someplace like that, see.

John T. Mason: What was your maximum depth?

Admiral McCain: Maximum depth would be around 317, 350 feet with the fleet-type submarine. But the S class—goddamn, I'd say 110, 120, something like that. Boy, I would hate to go deep in those things.

John T. Mason: Pretty vulnerable to depth charges.

Admiral McCain: Absolutely. We didn't use them during World War II.[*] It was the fleet-type submarine that I spoke to that did the job, and so forth.

But the training was good, though, regardless of what. And I keep going back again and again to you on this thing of leadership. We were constantly and continually

---

[*] Several S-boats did take part in combat early in World War II; others were used for training.

John S. McCain, Jr. (1/6/75) – Page 37

faced with the problems of leadership and doing the right job for the people that were subordinate to you, and doing the right sort of job that the captain of a submarine wanted above you, by the directions he'd given you. And, as I said again, the selective process in submarines was severe.

John T. Mason: There was very definitely a team, one cog in the slip, why, you were all lost.

Admiral McCain: That's right. You'd have troubles, to say the least. But, in any event, I went to the Skipjack, and then I went to New London. I think the war had gotten under way sometime in there, someplace. I went to New London to put the Gunnel in commission up there at Electric Boat Company in New London.*

John T. Mason: That was a little later now. Could we go back?

Admiral McCain: Yeah. [Interruption, tape recorder turned off] . . . during World War II came from the training that was given to them on S-boats.

John T. Mason: The caliber of personnel had its conception in the training on the S-boats.

Admiral McCain: That's right, had its foundation in its training.

John T. Mason: Now, Admiral Nimitz was very much interested in this area, was he not?†

Admiral McCain: Yes, he was very much interested in submarines. In the first place, he had a son who did an outstanding job in submarines, see. And Admiral Nimitz on

---

* USS Gunnel (SS-253) was a Gato-class submarine commissioned 20 August 1942. She had a displacement of 1,525 tons on the surface and 2,410 tons submerged. She was 312 feet long, 27 feet in the beam, and had a draft of 17 feet. Her top speed was 20 knots surfaced and 9 knots submerged. She was armed with ten 21-inch torpedo tubes and a 5-inch deck gun. McCain, then a lieutenant commander, was her first commanding officer.
† Fleet Admiral Chester W. Nimitz, USN, Commander in Chief Pacific Fleet and Pacific Ocean Areas, 1941-45. He had been a submariner earlier in his career.

occasions—I was never around there then, but I understand he went down to the dock to meet a submarine returning from war patrol, see. It's a unique life in submarines; there isn't any question about it. You're on your own, my friend. You get completely detached from the world.

John T. Mason: We go to the Naval Academy now, after your tour of duty on the S-class submarine. You came back to the Naval Academy rather than being sent to the Postgraduate School.

Admiral McCain: God bless those bunch of intellectuals. [Laughter] At the Naval Academy, when I went there, I reported in to the Department of Electrical Engineering and Physics—incidentally, one of those subjects that I very nearly failed at the Naval Academy when I was a midshipman myself. I immediately began to study and take this thing on. And then, as I say, the big thing was when old Captain Dessez came forward and said that during the academic year coming up, that the officers would alternate with the civilian professors on these lectures, and it fell to my lot—being the junior—to be the first one up. Of course, there was a civilian professor in particular there that was very popular with midshipmen. We used to call him "Slipstick Willie." He was there when I was a midshipman and later as an instructor, he was there when I came back.*

Professor Thomson—I don't know whatever happened to him either, but Thomson gave the first lecture, and it was my lot to give the second one. And these were two-hour lectures, my friend. This was no goddamn joke to sit up there and talk in front of a bunch of smart young fellows like these fellows were. They were no deadheads in that group. And another thing, nothing would please them more than to have a man in uniform, like a lieutenant such as I was, get up there and make some sort of a blunder or a bust.

And I got into the lecture, and I saw one of these young fellows half-asleep, so I stopped the lecture and I said, "Wake up." I said, "What's your name?" He told me what his name was. I said, "Well, you'll stand up the rest of the lecture." So then I went on and talked a bit, and, sure enough, I caught another one. Before I was through, there was

---

* "Slipstick Willie" was the nickname given Professor Earl W. Thomson because of his prowess with a slide rule. He taught at the Naval Academy from 1919 to 1959. For details see Shipmate magazine, published by the Naval Academy Alumni Association, June 1982, page 13.

someplace in the neighborhood of 15 of these young midshipmen standing up in various parts of the room while I finished the lecture. But I just want to say to you that they began to take a great interest in the lecture, too, from then on out.

John T. Mason: Was this technique something that just occurred to you?

Admiral McCain: It occurred to me as I stood up there. This gets into command, leadership, and all of the factors that go with it, see. And that's why I say I don't regret, in any sense, and did not regret after I got out of there of having been an instructor for two years. These young men are smart. They're in good health, they've had a good night's sleep, they eat three times a day with great regularity and everything else. They're ready to go. And you have to be on your toes if you're going to talk to them properly.

John T. Mason: I know.

Admiral McCain: Very much so. And I enjoyed every bit of it after that first lecture and got my own feet on the ground and had some sense of self-confidence.

John T. Mason: How often did you have to address the whole class?

Admiral McCain: Say about once every two months. So over a period, I did it, I'd say, 12 times, 15 times, something like that.

John T. Mason: Had you had any preparation in teaching techniques?

Admiral McCain: No.

John T. Mason: Any indoctrination?

Admiral McCain: No. I just got in there, and I tried to teach. I'm not one of these that belong to this great school that you have to have certain instructions in teaching techniques, either.

John T. Mason: Some of it comes naturally, doesn't it?

Admiral McCain: You either get up there and do it or you don't. And if you don't, you've got to get them out of there. Yes, it does come naturally. Of course, one of the points is, too, that whoever is doing the teaching has got to know his subject. You can't just get up there, because they'll trip you. When I was a midshipman, we were always busy seeing how we could trip the man who was standing up there in front, be he a professor or an officer, when I was a kid at the school.

But as I told you before, I am not one who believes in long, special courses in teaching, and I think it's a bunch of hogwash, if you want to know the truth. I've done a tremendous amount of speaking, instructing, talking, ordering, commanding, every damn thing you can think of. And the only thing I say to you is that you've got to know what you're talking about the moment you get up there.

John T. Mason: So this implies that you really knuckled in and did your homework in preparation for your teaching course.

Admiral McCain: You're damn right I did. And if you're interested to know why "force equals mass times acceleration," I can go right into that subject right now for you, my friend.

One of the big criteria of doing any of these things is knowing enough of the English language to be able to talk. Now, when I'm talking about knowing the English language, I'm not talking about a Spaniard learning the English language or anything. I'm talking about people that you and I know and like, having a sufficient vocabulary by virtue of their own reading, which is one of the most important aspects of it, and to get up and explain to people what they mean.

John T. Mason: Would you say something, too, about the value of experience, of taking back to the teaching the experience you had in the fleet?

Admiral McCain: Oh, yes, because by virtue of the fact that I had been in the fleet, in itself has an impact on these young men sitting in front of you. This is the place they know the least about. This is the place that the great majority of them will go, but also being in the fleet, you understand the importance of the job that you've been assigned as an instructor, in talking to these young people. And it comes through loud and clear to you when you get up there and talk to them, self-consciously or consciously. Suddenly—I won't say suddenly. I'll say you realize fully the responsibility that you carry, and you also realize that the very impact that you have on them, by virtue of your personal appearance—and your uniform ought to look well, your shoes ought to be shined, and I will now use "damn" in all of its aspects, your damned hair ought to be cut, and things of this sort, see. The whole thing intermeshes.

John T. Mason: So you came from the fleet. You have, in a sense, an advantage over the civilian instructor, then, do you not?

Admiral McCain: Oh, no, I don't think so. Maybe in one sense that you come from the fleet, but also don't forget the civilian instructor has been there year after year after year. And if he is a good civilian professor, he will have kept himself alert and awake to all of the changing facets of modern physics. And these subjects are not static. In fact, I don't know any subject in life that's static right now. And I know that when I was a midshipman at the Naval Academy, there were some civilian and there were some military that we had great respect for and appreciated being in their sections. It didn't make any difference whether they wore the uniform or not.

One point I want to make in going to the Naval Academy as an instructor, I had wanted, really, to go to the PG School.

John T. Mason: Oh, so you had wanted to do that?

Admiral McCain: So I thought at that time, see.

John T. Mason: But it was the thing to do in the development of a career.

Admiral McCain: That's right. And it was the thing that carried the greatest weight with the detail officer back in the Bureau of Naval Personnel, was whether you had been to one of these schools or not.[*] But, again, I want to say and repeat that you can make anything out of any job that you want to make, as you go into it.

I had a strange assignment right after World War II. They brought me back and put me in charge of the records activity in the Bureau of Naval Personnel. And there were something like one million enlisted men records, and I forget how many officer records, see. But there was a backlog of filing of papers into these records in the neighborhood of several million sheets. And when you get into several million of anything, you're getting into real problems of management.

And I had a team up there of 500 sailors, 300 or 400 WAVES.[†] I had all sorts of organizations and everything else. And the last place on earth I thought I'd ever be ordered to in my life was to take care of records in the Bureau of Naval Personnel. I must admit it's an interesting job, because you read all sorts of strange things about people that you don't ordinarily get your hands on, see, and so forth.

But after I left that job, I went back to sea in command of a division of submarines, which was good, but none of these jobs in any sense deterred my future. In fact, they greatly aided and abetted. And a big point is to go into the job as though this is one of the best things that's ever happened, see.

John T. Mason: And not let it defeat you.

---

[*] Prior to World War II, assignments of naval officers were made by the Bureau of Navigation. On 13 May 1942, it became the Bureau of Naval Personnel (BuPers), a title that better described its function.
[†] The WAVES (Women Accepted for Volunteer Emergency Service) were established by law on 30 July 1942. From then until the early 1970s, when women ceased to be designated as a separate branch of the Navy, the term was still used.

Admiral McCain: That's right. And, goddamn, if some customer sits up and says something about it, tell them, "Boy, I wouldn't want to be behind that desk where you are," I wouldn't have been. I was my own boss up there. My God, I had 1,500 enlisted men under my command, I had 500 civil service under my command up in that area, with all the problems that went with it. And this then goes back to leadership, it goes back to command, it goes back to organization, it goes back to administration and all the rest of these things that distinguished gentlemen write about in big, weighty volumes about how you do the job, see.

John T. Mason: So you were initially disappointed that you didn't get assigned to PG School.

Admiral McCain: Right.

John T. Mason: You soon lost this feeling.

Admiral McCain: Yes, I didn't—the disappointment wasn't something that lasted any length of time.

John T. Mason: Well, it was two years.

Admiral McCain: Yes, but I wasn't unhappy, to tell you the truth of the matter.

John T. Mason: You weren't unhappy at all with the teaching process.

Admiral McCain: And my God. Listen, I graduated from the Naval Academy at the age of 20. This was the age of 26 or 27. My God, you don't get unhappy at that age unless you're a damn fool. I had a lot of things I was doing in life.

John T. Mason: Were you married at that point?

Admiral McCain: Yeah, but I was also working on a special gadget that I had devised my own, of firing torpedoes from bearings alone.

John T. Mason: Tell me about this.

Admiral McCain: Well, it's too goddamn complicated.

John T. Mason: No, no.

Admiral McCain: They've gotten into systems now that far exceed it, but it was a stunt that whereby by just taking bearings on a target like this, when you're running submerged and can't see him through the periscope, by just taking bearings on them and knowing your own course and speed, and making an estimate of his, can get sufficient derivation of his range and course. You fire a torpedo at him on sound bearings alone with a good possibility of hitting and sinking him. That's what the thing was. I used to call the goddamn thing a Ouiji board, but I used to work on that all the time.

John T. Mason: What inspired this originally in you?

Admiral McCain: The fact that, goddamn, we didn't have any way of doing it. Then later on all the PG characters from ordnance—it didn't actually come from there. The ordnance laboratory, I guess, down here at the Washington Navy Yard and places like that really began to work on this problem after that. At least it stimulated that much, see.

John T. Mason: And you were doing this while you were teaching at the academy? You were working on this idea.

Admiral McCain: I was working on it before I even got there. And I was also working on another stunt before I got there. We used to have guns on submarines, and the only way you could fire the gun was by pushing a foot pedal, which in turn released the firing pin, which in turn fired the shell, see. But when you pushed on the foot pedal, the pressure that it took to do so had a tendency to throw the pointer off—the man who was firing. When I say pointer, I'm speaking of the man, now, firing the gun. It had a tendency to throw him off because he has to apply the pressure.

John T. Mason: So the accuracy was lost.

Admiral McCain: That's right. So I went ahead and devised a solenoid with an electrical device to it that all he had to do was push the little button in his right hand. The solenoid would pull up like that, which in turn then would release the firing pin and the shell would be shot, and so forth. But there were all sorts of things like that I was doing all my life, see, on these things.

John T. Mason: That's one aspect of your creativity I knew nothing about, I mean, the inventor in you.

Admiral McCain: I wouldn't call it inventor. Anyway, it was things like that. I spent a great deal of time in that records activity when I was over there at the Bureau of Naval Personnel, working on a method of the selection of officers for high command that selected them on the basis of their capabilities from a command view rather than because they could fly a plane, dive a submarine or steer a destroyer. And there still isn't a good system, I want to tell you that, because they don't want to do it. The aviators are jealous of their position, submariners are jealous of their position, and so forth, see. But I worked on that in this training and education for high command. That was another aspect of it. Things like that all through, see.

The only time I haven't worked on things like these, this sort of thing I'm talking to you about, is when I actually moved into high command, where I was so goddamn busy initiating other actions along other lines to keep the enemy off dead center, that I didn't have a chance to get as specific as I'm talking to you now about these other areas.

John T. Mason: All this demonstrates a very fertile and active imagination, however.

Admiral McCain: Somebody has got to get on with the business of getting across to the public about this thing of the grave dangers we face worldwide. And Kissinger is one of the greatest.*

---

* Henry A. Kissinger was the President's national security adviser, 1969-73 and later served as Secretary of State, 1973-77.

HOLD FOR RELEASE 10:30 a.m. 3 June

COMMENCEMENT ADDRESS TO THE 1970 GRADUATING CLASS OF MIDSHIPMEN, UNITED STATES NAVAL ACADEMY, ANNAPOLIS, MARYLAND, BY ADMIRAL JOHN S. McCAIN, Jr., USN, COMMANDER IN CHIEF PACIFIC

WEDNESDAY, 3 JUNE 1970

Exactly 39 years ago to the day, on the 3rd of June 1931, I sat where you are now with the expectations of youth and the stamp of the U. S. Naval Academy indelibly impressed on my character. And to save my life as I stand before you now I cannot remember who gave the graduation address for the Class of 1931. I hope you may manifest a somewhat higher span of attention and that I will make a more lasting impression on you.

You have just finished four years of intense study and training such as you will never experience again. There are those amongst you whose future intentions may include transferring to the other services or returning to civilian life as soon as circumstances permit.

To those who leave the service the schooling and training you have received will stand you in good stead. To those who stay, the Naval Academy trains the professional.

Your country expects you to take this schooling and serve the Nation to the extreme limits of your ability. There are times when this service will lead you into the valley of the shadow of death. And for some, unto death itself. I have friends and classmates who gave their lives that the citizens of the United States would be free to live lives of their own choosing, which includes your freedom to choose to become a Midshipman.

ADM McCain.....2222

The greatest tribute that can be paid to the United States Naval Academy is recognition of the long succession of naval officers who have passed through these gates and have gone forth to give their lives for freedom. The historic battles in which they fought are recorded on both sides of this beautiful stadium. Their names are memorialized on plaques on the back of seats now occupied by your families and friends. These officers were imbued with a sense of loyalty and dedication that scorns vacillation and doubt. From your class, the class of 1970, will come the heroes of tomorrow. Sitting here in front of me are those who in keeping with the highest traditions of the Naval service will make the greatest sacrifice that a man can make for his Country.

This, gentlemen, is your heritage. You have been exposed to traditions that ultimately will become a part of your character. You will not question where your duty lies.

Today as so often in the past we are living in a troubled world. We are at war far from home under difficult and complex circumstances. Our leaders seek an early and honorable end to the struggle. There is reason for hope and measured optimism. One of the great acts of moral courage and discipline in this search for peace was when President Nixon ordered the execution of the Cambodian operation. This campaign has met our fondest hopes.

It has set back the enemy time table. The resources the Chinese Communists and the Russians are willing to divert and the problems of transportation have great bearing on this time table. The U. S. went into Cambodia to protect allied forces by destroying enemy sanctuaries. We did just this. By 30 June we will be out.

ADM McCAIN....3333

We have taken caches consisting of millions of rounds of small arms ammunition, over 5000 tons of rice and thousands of weapons. To give you some idea of the amount of captured rice, it would have fed over 15,000 North Vietnamese and Viet Cong for one year on a full ration. Even though the Communists return to the sanctuaries it will take them 5-10 months to bring in arms, ammunition and supplies to resume the same level of action. By this time the South Vietnamese Armed Forces will be in a better position to take over.

In South Vietnam the story is the same. The President's policy is sound and the current plan for withdrawal of 150,000 men is both safe and reasonable, particularly in view of our success in Cambodia.

CHALLENGES TO PEACE

However, I hasten to caution you that peace in Southeast Asia or elsewhere is not just around the corner. The challenges for the military officer have never been greater and service to country never more meaningful. The expanding projection of Soviet power world-wide through military, political, psychological, and economic means is well publicized.

<u>First</u> of all, and of particular importance to you fine young naval officers we honor here today, is the challenge provided by the recent emergence of Soviet seapower throughout the oceans of the world.

<u>Secondly</u>, there is the problem of the border conflict between Russia and mainland China, both Communist nations. It may appear on the surface that the United States has no interest in this dispute but we do. If war should come to these two nations, the rest of the

world will be affected if not drawn in to the vortex of this conflagration. We must continually guard against actions on the part of either Red China or Russia which by design or accident entangle or embarrass us.

<u>Third</u>, there is the very dangerous situation that exists in the Middle East.

<u>Fourth</u>, is the continuing question of the two Germany's.

<u>Fifth</u>, is the conflict in Southeast Asia.

<u>And finally</u>, the Strategic Arms Limitation Talks in Vienna are a forum in which the United States and Soviet Russia confront each other over critically important interests at the conference table.

THE STRONG MAN ARMED

It is apparent that the United States must maintain a strong military and political posture in the world if we are to survive. This means a strong Army and Air Force, a strong Navy and Marine Corps. Although concerned with all four, the primary interest of most of you for the near future will be the Navy and Marine Corps.

The Navy and Marine Corps bring a mobile base philosophy to the defense establishment that applies directly to over three quarters of the earth's surface. One of the most profound changes in the history of warfare and yet little recognized has been the inland reach of naval power. The aircraft carrier, the polaris submarine, the amphibious capability of the Navy-Marine Corps Team are outstanding examples. The profession in which you have been and will continue to be trained involves every aspect of modern warfare--land, sea, and air. Today the Nixon Doctrine places increasing emphasis upon the mobile forces of our entire military establishment.

ADM McCAIN....5555

As you embark on the profession of arms the single most important factor in reaching your objective is an understanding of the basic role of the Bluejacket and the enlisted Marine. This applies equally to the Soldier and the Airman. The highest accomplishment that an officer can achieve is mastering the art of leadership which means the ability to inspire the enlisted men to the highest performance of duty, particularly under enemy fire.

I now want to discuss the art of leadership. There is no "Masters Degree in Leadership." It does not lend itself to a mathematical formula recognized by certificate of diploma. It is above this. Although the greater number of us can never rise to the heights of John Paul Jones, David Glasgow Farragut, Ernest Joseph King and others, there are certain principles that act as buoys clearly marking the channel beyond which you are in trouble.

QUALITIES OF LEADERSHIP

As each man seeks his own way to heaven so each officer develops his own method of leadership. When you step aboard ship and stand in front of your first division of Bluejackets they will evaluate you accurately and without delay. In fact there is no more exacting method of determining an officer's worth. Furthermore you can't fool Bluejackets. They are quick to recognize the phony. If you lose the respect of these men, you are finished, you never regain it.

When you become a Commanding Officer, air, surface or subsurface, you are working at what has been referred to as the courtmartial level. You are held strictly accountable for your command. You are the only one who can make the ultimate decisions. By the same token, you are the one who must bear the responsibility for failure. When

ADM McCAIN....6666

matters go wrong you are the one who is subject to possible court-martial. Thus and properly so, the road to high command is hard, tough and demands the highest of human qualities.

A mark of greatness is willingness to listen. In fact one commits a grave error who fails to seek advice. I listen to any member of my staff regardless of rank or rate. One of the most difficult problems to solve is the reticence of subordinates to speak out in the presence of seniors. To a certain degree this stems from custom and tradition which should not restrict the junior at the appropriate time. To surmount this barrier takes time and patience. If a seaman on the foc'sle says there is something dead ahead, I stop the ship to find out.

There is an expression, "officer and gentleman," and it applies as fully today as it did one hundred years ago. In fact, under the circumstances today that tend to degrade values of the past it becomes even more important. To quote John Paul Jones, "A gentleman is one who has the nicest sense of personal honor." His instincts are of such a high order that he never unintentionally hurts another person. This does not mean that he can't and won't if it becomes necessary to do so. In the days of the square rigger the oncoming officer of the deck in applying the code of an officer and gentleman made it a point not to change the set of the sails for the first fifteen minutes of his watch out of deference to his shipmate whom he had just relieved. Obviously certain conditions of wind and sea might require a departure from this rule. An officer must be prepared to move with equal ease as officer of the deck or in the highest and most complex diplomatic circles. The social graces are as much a part of his life as the

ADM McCAIN....7777

rules of seamanship. These are requirements which remain unchanged through the centuries.

VALUE OF INITIATIVE

As you execute your duties, another attribute to cultivate is initiative. This trait is invaluable but also can lead to real trouble if not balanced with judgment and common sense. In this connection the regulations are to guide and not fetter the judgment. The only time I studied the regulations was in time of trouble. However I repeat that each officer must find his own way to effective leadership. The detail and style of leadership varies from one man to the next as much as the character and personality of two individuals.

The Naval Academy has subjected you to continual exposure to discipline which today is little appreciated in so many circles. Discipline is a basic and an indispensable element of success. The art of leadership and discipline are synonymous. No man is worth his salt without self-discipline. If you cannot discipline yourself you can rest assured that you will fail where others are concerned. He who lacks self-discipline cannot command.

This trait is equally important in the civilian world. You know of those signs that say "make love not war." You belong to a fraternity whose members are men enough to do both.

In this regard, the fact that you have earned your commissions is ample evidence that you are dedicated to the preservation of our values and institutions. This is in direct contrast to those we read about in the newspapers who preach destruction of the fabric of our society often without even the vaguest concept of what kind of structure and value system would replace it.

ADM McCAIN....8888

I once heard a distinguished gentleman say that the world consists of two broad categories of men, the S.O.B.'s and the good fellows. The good fellows are always helping each other up the ladder to success. But the S.O.B., you have to give him full credit, he got there on his own two feet. Your career as a leader falls somewhere between these two. It is just as bad to be a popularity jack as it is to be a S.O.B. You must be fair and square. You must be consistent.

HUMAN RELATIONS AND THE GOLDEN RULE

The cardinal principle of leadership is the Golden Rule - "do unto others as you would have them do unto you." It takes moral courage to issue an unpopular order and then to make sure of its execution. In this regard a policy of permissiveness at sea does not work any more than it does any other place in the world. A good officer instead of telling the crew that the Captain wants a certain order carried out executes in his own name without leaning on higher authority.

Men who have faced danger do not have to be introduced to religion. It has been said there are no athiests in a fox hole. Although I have never been in a fox hole, I spent my wartime years in a submarine and know that nothing makes a man turn more quickly to God than the uncertainties of battle. The brave man needs no lesson, while the coward thinks with his feet. I believe in God. He answers prayers. Never be afraid to acknowledge belief in a higher power. The profession upon which you are entering is dangerous and exciting. God is ever present.

In a few moments you will be sworn in as commissioned officers. You will take an oath to defend the Constitution of the United States of America and with this goes an obligation that is a privilege

ADM McCAIN....9999

accorded to relatively few. Some of you may not understand the full import of this statement. In time you will. It means hard work, long watches, hours of flying, hours of fighting in swamps, heavy seas, and so on ad infinitum. You are on duty 24 hours a day.

You are about to become guardians of a great legacy. One handed down to you by generations of Americans, dedicated men and women, who placed their nation's welfare above personal ambition. The proud responsibility which you will share in passing on to a new generation our priceless values and institutions will continue to give quality and meaning to the American tradition.

Gentlemen, you are about the join the most exacting and honorable profession in the world. The future of the Country will rest in your hands. I am proud of the United States Navy. I am proud of you. God Bless each and everyone!

Index to the Oral History of
Admiral John S. McCain, Jr.,
U.S. Navy (Retired)

Alcohol
  During the late 1920s and early 1930s some Naval Academy midshipmen availed themselves of a speakeasy in Annapolis, 22

Ammon, Lieutenant William B., USN (USNA, 1923)
  Did a fine job in the early 1930s while serving in the communication department of the battleship Oklahoma (BB-37), 27-28

Bureau of Naval Personnel, Arlington, Virginia
  Record-keeping function in the years following World War II, 42-43; selection of officers for command, 45

Columbia Preparatory School, Washington, D.C.
  Run by a man named Shadman, it had a fine program in the 1920s for preparing young men to enter the Naval Academy and Military Academy, 2-3, 9

Communications
  On board the battleship Oklahoma (BB-37) in the early 1930s, 27-28

Dessez, Captain John H. S., USN (USNA, 1909)
  Served in the late 1930s as chairman of electrical engineering and physics at the Naval Academy, 12, 38

Discipline
  During the late 1920s and early 1930s some Naval Academy midshipmen ran afoul of rules and regulations, 21-22

Fire Control
  In the 1930s McCain devised methods for aiming torpedoes and submarine deck guns, 44-45

Gunnery-Naval
  In the 1930s McCain developed a method for firing deck guns on submarines, 44-45

Holloway, Admiral James L. III, USN (USNA, 1943)
  Assessment by Admiral John S. McCain, Jr., of Holloway's tenure in the mid-1970s as Chief of Naval Operations, 18

Leadership
  McCain's philosophy on, 13-14, 36-37

McCain, Admiral John S., USN (Ret.) (USNA, 1906)
Various naval duties during the boyhood of his son, John, Jr., 1, 4-5; personal qualities of, 5-6; last visit with his son on board the submarine tender Proteus (AS-19) in September 1945 in Tokyo Bay, 5-6; death of on 6 September 1945, 6; encouraged his son to play golf, 15-16; career advice to his son, 29

McCain, Admiral John S., Jr., USN (Ret.) (USNA, 1931)
Parents of, 1, 4-6, 15-16, 22, 29; boyhood and education of in the 1910s and 1920s, 1-4; personal qualities of, 5; last visit with his father on board the submarine tender Proteus (AS-19) in September 1945 in Tokyo Bay, 5-6; spent 1927-31 as a midshipman at the Naval Academy, 7-26; concern about personal honor, 9-11, 18-19, 24; delivered the 1970 graduation address at the Naval Academy, 13; philosophy on leadership, 13-14; served from 1968 to 1972 as Commander in Chief Pacific, 20-21; son John S. McCain III was a prisoner of war in Vietnam, 21; rapid pulse disqualified him from flight training, 26-27; service from 1931 to 1933 in the crew of the battleship Oklahoma (BB-37), 27-28, 30; in the late 1930s served as a physics instructor at the Naval Academy, 28-29, 38-41; as a student in 1933 at submarine school, 32-33; duty in the late 1940s in the Bureau of Naval Personnel, 42, 45

McCain, Captain John S. III, USN (Ret.) (USNA, 1958)
Spent the period from 1967 to 1973 as a prisoner of war in Vietnam, 21

Naval Academy, Annapolis, Maryland
Training program in the 1927-31 period for midshipmen, 7-11; hazing, 8-9; academics in the 1920s and 1930s, 12, 28-29, 38-41; McCain delivered the 1970 graduation address at the academy, 13; in the 1970s the academy ended compulsory chapel attendance for midshipmen, 14-15; athletics in the late 1920s, 15; summer cruises, 16-19; disciplinary problems, 21-22; during the late 1920s and early 1930s some midshipmen availed themselves of a speakeasy in Annapolis, 22; social life for midshipmen, 23; training of midshipmen in writing and in public speaking, 25

Nimitz, Fleet Admiral Chester W., USN (USNA, 1905)
Interest in submarines and submariners while serving in World War II as Commander in Chief Pacific Fleet, 37-38

Oklahoma, USS (BB-37)
Shipboard communication department in the early 1930s, 27-28; operation of aircraft catapults, 28; junior officers' mess, 30; operations of the ship in the early 1930s, 30-31

Pearl Harbor, Hawaii, Naval Base
In the early 1930s its facilities were limited in scope, 31

Personnel
    Record-keeping function in the Bureau of Naval Personnel in the years following World War II, 42-43; selection of officers for command, 45

Prisoners of War
    From 1967 to 1973 John S. McCain III was a prisoner of war in Vietnam, 21

Proteus, USS (AS-19)
    Submarine tender that on 2 September 1945 served as the site of a meeting between Vice Admiral John S. McCain and his son, John, Jr., 5-6

Religion
    Compulsory chapel attendance ended in the 1970s for Naval Academy midshipmen, 14-15

S-45, USS (SS-156)
    Submarine that operated out of Hawaii in the mid-1930s, 31, 35-38

Shadman School
    See: Columbia Preparatory School, Washington, D.C.

Soviet Navy
    Rise in power and capability in the 1960s and 1970s, 24-25

Submarines
    Curriculum to train prospective submariners in the early 1930s at the submarine school in New London, 32-33; development in the 1930s of fleet-type boats, 34-36; in the 1930s McCain developed devices for firing torpedoes and shipboard guns, 44-45

Submarine School, New London, Connecticut
    Curriculum to train prospective submariners in the early 1930s, 32-33

Thomson, Professor Earl W.
    Known by the nickname "Slipstick Willie," he taught for many years at the Naval Academy, 38

Torpedoes
    In the 1930s McCain devised a gadget for firing torpedoes from submarines, 44

Training
    Curriculum for students at submarine school in the early 1930s, 32-33

Vietnam War
As Commander in Chief Pacific from 1968 to 1972, McCain often visited U.S. forces that were in country in Vietnam, 20; McCain's views on the war, 20-21 John S. McCain III was a prisoner of war in Vietnam, 21

Zumwalt, Admiral Elmo R., Jr., USN (USNA, 1943)
His reforms as Chief of Naval Operations in the early 1970s did not sit well with many senior officers, 18

www.ingramcontent.com/pod-product-compliance
Lightning Source LLC
Chambersburg PA
CBHW080609170426
43209CB00007B/1383